Gathered for God

VOLUME 8
in the
Church's Teachings for a Changing World
series

JEFFREY LEE AND DENT DAVIDSON

Church Publishing
NEW YORK

Church Publishing
19 East 34th Street
New York, NY 10016
www.churchpublishing.org

Cover art: *Heaven's Door* by Tim Steward
Cover design by Laurie Klein Westhafer, Bounce Design
Typeset by Beth Oberholtzer

Library of Congress Cataloging-in-Publication Data

Names: Lee, Jeffrey D., 1957– author.
Title: Gathered for God / Jeffrey Lee and Dent Davidson.
Description: New York : Church Publishing, 2018. | Series: The church's teachings for a changing world series ; Volume 8 | Includes bibliographical references.
Identifiers: LCCN 2017044227 (print) | LCCN 2017046957 (ebook) | ISBN
  9780898690446 (ebook) | ISBN 9780898690439 (pbk.)
Subjects: LCSH: Public worship—Episcopal Church.
Classification: LCC BX5940 (ebook) | LCC BX5940 .L436 2018 (print) | DDC
  264/.03—dc23
LC record available at https://lccn.loc.gov/2017044227

Printed in the United States of America

Contents

Preface

One of the ways God is revealed to human beings is through the gift of friendship. The Bible describes a moment in the life of Jesus when he tells his first group of followers this: "I do not call you servants any longer, because the servant does not know what the master is doing; but I have called you friends, because I have made known to you everything that I have heard from my Father" (John 15:15).

The authors of this book have been friends and colleagues for almost twenty years. We worked together in a congregation—St. Thomas Episcopal Church in Medina, Washington—and are now the bishop of the Episcopal Diocese of Chicago (Jeff) and its chief liturgical officer (Dent). We share a love of music and a passion (some of our friends would say "obsession") with good food. Our families often share holidays and special occasions at each other's tables. We laugh at each other's jokes and make space for our differences.

Above all, in our friendship we have discovered important convictions about the presence of God in our lives and in the lives of the people we serve and also call friends. We believe that at its best the church can be a place of life-changing encounter with the vast and intimate mystery of God.

Here are just a few things we have learned from each other, and why we are grateful to collaborate on this unique venture.

Jeff

Dent is a remarkable musician. His sheer command of musical styles and idioms is a wonder—from classical to contemporary to global music and jazz. In church, he weaves together resources from all these traditions into seamless occasions of sound and song.

And yet, as any number of people who have sung in choirs under his direction or played with him in ensembles or worshiped in congregations with his leadership can tell you, the most remarkable thing about Dent's work is not its techniques or details. It is his transparent delight in the act of making music in praise of God.

Dent has taught me the importance of freedom, that "offering our best" to God in worship has less to do with perfection than with the willingness to offer our sometimes ragged hearts in song, silence and wonder. He has increased my reverence for the profound holiness of what happens when a group of people comes together to sing and celebrate the mystery we call God. When he steps before a congregation on a Sunday morning to teach us a new song and calls out, "Good morning, church!" somehow, we know that we are exactly that—church. We are the people of God, gathered for something extraordinary that's about to happen.

Dent

My first encounter with Jeff left a lasting impression that made me want to work with him. It was one of those sparkling Pacific Northwest days: Mount Rainier commanded the view to the south as we crossed Puget Sound on a ferry, playful pilot whales adding joy to the occasion. We talked about what we might do for dinner, and there was no question we'd be cooking together. And after a trip to Pike Place Market, what a dinner we had.

Since that time, Jeff has been a mentor, a friend, a colleague and a companion on the way. I continue to be deeply formed in my own faith as I work alongside him, watching, listening, anticipating. It is through his leadership that I have learned the art of presiding, especially how he exhibits a gracious, non-anxious attention as worship unfolds. His preaching is *par excellence*: uplifting, challenging, relatable messages that are always centered in the heart of God's love, best witnessed in the dying and rising of Jesus.

He makes the act of planning liturgy one of joy and openness to what new things God might have to say, to us as leaders, and to the Church and the world. He knows that liturgy is one of the best ways to empower the Church to share God's love beyond our doors; and his commitment to forming a vital, vibrant church, is an essential part of transforming the world around us.

Ultimately, Jeff models the dream of God: the inclusion of all people as the waters of baptism wash us and unite us and send us into the world like a flood to be the people of God.

Jeff and Dent

Together, we want to thank our families for their love, patience and support as we worked on this book. Truly, the family is the domestic church. We thank series editor The Rev. Canon Stephanie Spellers for her trust in us that we might have something useful to say about the Episcopal way of worship and for her constant and wise encouragement. We benefitted, too, from the generous expertise and advice of Rebecca Wilson in putting together this text.

We give thanks to God for the wonderful communities we have served together and for the people who have shaped us both in the service and praise of God, especially St. Mark's Cathedral, Seattle; St. Thomas Episcopal Church, Medina; and the many people of God in the Diocese of Chicago. We have learned from them all that the Christian life is not a performance, but a daily practice of love and service and praise. We are grateful beyond words for the many ways we have known the abundance of God's love and mercy as we have gathered with them.

Introduction

We were on our way back from a long relay race. In the back of the van I was having a conversation with my twenty-four-year-old teammate, an intern living in a house with six peers as part of the Episcopal Service Corps. He and his young adult peers commit to a year of living in prayerful community, working with people in need, and engaging in public action toward a more just society.

My teammate had discovered the Episcopal Church in college when a friend invited him. "It was the way they worshiped," he said. "I mean, I walked into that place and there was this priest, holding a chalice and saying things like, 'This is my blood.' I was blown away. That's like straight out of *Game of Thrones*."

Popular culture is no stranger to themes of light and shadow, good and evil, salvation and loss, mystery and symbol. Movies and television, popular music, novels, websites—it's not difficult to find lots of material having at least something to do with our longing for meaning, even when it is cloaked in the trappings of escapist entertainment. In a society that runs by the logic of disposability and consumerism—remember: "You are what you buy!"—many people are hungry for something more. Much more.

Ultimately, human beings are hungry for God. **Sacramental Christianity**—a way of expressing our faith through ritual and liturgy—explores this fundamental hunger. In the particular way of being Christian we have received in the Episcopal Church, there is a powerful set of practices that not only help us understand our ultimate hunger, but also begin to address the physical and spiritual hungers of others in this world.

> The Book of Common Prayer defines a **sacrament** as an outward and visible sign of an inward and spiritual grace. But another way to think about that definition is that sacraments like baptism and communion are actions that give new meaning to things.[1]

The most obvious and public of these practices happen in worship. The guidebook for our worship is **The Book of Common Prayer**. You'll find copies in the seats or pews of most any Episcopal church, although the forms in it (or other material produced by the church as supplements to it) might be printed in a booklet for ease of use. The prayer book represents a long tradition that goes back to the English Ref-

---

1. Bernard Cooke, *Sacraments & Sacramentality* (Mystic, CT: Twenty-Third Publications, 2006).

ormation in the 1500s and really much earlier. It is a kind of living record of the way Christians have worshiped for a very long time (perhaps to a time much more like *Game of Thrones*), and it points to how that way continues to evolve.

There are lots of resources for exploring the history, development and shape of the Book of Common Prayer. Rest assured, we'll provide a suggested list of some of them later. But this book is not primarily about the Book of Common Prayer; it's about what the Book of Common Prayer is *for*.

When we gather for worship, it is not simply to share some interesting ideas about God or fond theories regarding what we might make of Jesus. We gather in the presence of God. We gather to meet, to receive, to share in the life, death, and resurrection of Jesus himself. And we do this the way he taught us by his own example: at table, in the breaking and sharing of bread, in a cup of wine, passed from hand to hand.

Chapter 1

Gathered for Ritual

The most common act of worship you are likely to experience in the Episcopal Church is the **Holy Eucharist**. The word *eucharist* means "thanksgiving." On any given Sunday in most Episcopal churches, you will find a group of people giving thanks over a simple meal of bread and wine. Christians have done this in some form from the earliest days. In fact, biblical stories that try to convey that Jesus is alive often describe people sharing a meal.

None of this is surprising. Jesus was a real human being. He learned and laughed and cried and taught and loved and got in trouble with those in power and finally suffered an agonizing death. He ate and drank with all kinds of people, often offending the rigid sensibilities of his day about who was acceptable or not. After his crucifixion, the community of friends and followers that had gathered around him did the same things. They continued to share the meal where Jesus had promised to gather with them.

Back to Emmaus

One of the most precious stories in the Bible is about two friends of Jesus who left Jerusalem on the afternoon of his resurrection, headed to a place called Emmaus (Luke 24:13–35). Were they trying to get out of Dodge? Were they afraid the authorities might come after them next? Were they just trying to escape their grief that Jesus was gone?

We don't know, but Luke tells us that as they walked along swapping stories, a "stranger" comes alongside them, somebody who knows nothing of the stories they share. "Are you the only person who's been in Jerusalem who doesn't know what's happened?" they ask. "What things?" says the stranger. The story turns almost comical here, a little giddy. They tell him all about Jesus and what has happened, their hopes and dreams about him, the possibility that he was the one to rescue them from the terrible oppression of all that imperial Rome represented, and now all of that is dashed on the cross.

The story goes on. It's getting dark. They come to an inn and beg this stranger to come join them. Suddenly, the table starts to turn. The stranger they've invited to be their guest suddenly becomes their host. He takes the bread, breaks it, and with stunning speed, they get it. Jesus has been walking with them all this way, unrecognized. It wasn't their ideas that revealed him. It wasn't some miracle, nor was it some test they passed. It was the action of breaking open that loaf. It was the breaking open of their lives.

Those two would never be the same again. The story says they got up and ran back to the one place in all the world they probably thought they would never see again: Jerusalem. They went back to the scene of their grief and despair, back to the other friends of Jesus with the message that grief and despair isn't all there is. They went back with a word of hope. They went back with a bewildering experience of joy and a growing conviction that there isn't any hunger God can't fill.

Emmaus is the pattern for what still goes on in church, what happens whenever Christians gather to break bread. In the Holy Land, six miles or so outside Jerusalem, there is a town named Abu Ghosh. It is one of the traditional sites that many Christians through the centuries have identified as the biblical Emmaus. In Abu Ghosh there is a remarkable church building that dates from the Crusader era. Named the Church of the Resurrection, it is now part of a Benedictine monastery.

One of the church's most striking features is its interior walls, which are covered with hauntingly beautiful frescoes, images of biblical scenes, angels and saints. There is a mysterious air about these frescoes because most of the faces have been erased. They were removed when the building was held by Muslim believers, since Islam prohibits any visual portrayals of God or saints

To gather for the Eucharist in this church today is to be surrounded by the faceless images of ancient, faithful people. Standing there, you have the sense that these people could be anyone, including us. We are, after all, living the pattern they laid out all those centuries ago.

A Container for the Holy

While we can't know precisely what happened in these earliest experiences, we do know these encounters were so powerful that in some sense they launched the whole Christian movement. The first Christians kept the meal that had transformed their lives and allowed it to take a particular shape. Regular, repeatable gestures, prayers, stories, even the way the food itself is shared—all of that can be described under the heading of **ritual**. Ritual exists to provide a container for an experience of the holy—something that may have taken your breath away—so that others might encounter it, too. Ritual is the art of inviting people to be changed.

We call Christian ritual **liturgy**. The Greek word *leitourgia* meant something like a public work at private expense. In ancient Greece for instance the *leitourgia* referred to public service performed by wealthy citizens for the sake of the common good.

Today in church you will often hear the word liturgy defined as the "work of the people." This definition is usu-

Originally, the Greek word from which we get the word **liturgy** could refer to public service performed by wealthy citizens for the sake of the common good.

ally aimed at reminding worshipers that every member of a worshiping assembly has a part to play, an active role in making the act of worship happen. In the Episcopal Church, as in other liturgical churches, worship is not just about the preacher and whatever edifying thing he or she may have to say. It's not all about *the* minister. Rather, there are many ministers: readers, musicians, distributers of the bread and wine, ushers, priests, deacons, and more. It takes all of them to make this public offering.

This is why it is increasingly common to hear Episcopalians talk about the priest who is leading an act of worship as the **presider**. The Book of Common Prayer uses the term "celebrant" for this person, but in a real sense, every person who attends the gathering is a celebrant—we are all celebrating this liturgy—or more accurately, it is Christ himself celebrating it in and through his people. We all celebrate; one of us presides.

This dynamic relationship is clear in the dialogue at the opening of the prayer over the bread and wine:

Priest: The Lord be with you.

People: And also with you.

Priest: Lift up your hearts.

People: We lift them to the Lord.

Priest: Let us give thanks to the Lord.

People: It is right to give God thanks and praise.

This dialogue is like a series of questions and answers between priest and people. In effect, the priest is asking the permission of the whole assembly to continue the prayer in its name. When the people say or sing "Amen" (which may be related to a Hebrew word meaning truthfulness) at the end of the whole prayer, they are affirming the truth of what has been prayed. We might translate Amen as "So be it." This ritual meal takes the whole congregation to make it so.

Making Believe

Ritual is the subject of this book. We are made for ritual. Human beings are symbol-making creatures. If we don't have healthy rituals, we will invent others, good or bad. Think of the highly ritualized behaviors of the professional football game, or the elaborate symbols and initiation rites of sororities and fraternities or the alarming rituals of urban gang culture. Ritual is part of being human.

Christian ritual, the liturgy of the church, is meant to be an invitation to an encounter with the dying and rising Christ, an encounter that can change us and send us to do God's work in the world. While Christians have no exclusive claim on how God chooses to be revealed in this world, we believe that this encounter and this possibility happens reliably, according to the promise of Jesus, in the midst of those who have been made members of Christ's Body through the water of baptism (more on this in chapters 2 and 8).

The Episcopal way of being Christian is a very practical one. We do not ask people to believe (more on *that* word too a little later) elaborate ideas about God or the Bible or Jesus before they can be counted members. To belong to the Episcopal Church you must simply do what the church does. The church gathers; that's what the word "church" means. The word "**church**" in the Bible comes from the Greek word *ecclesia,* from which we get words like "ecclesiastical." It means "to be called out," as a gathering. And when the church gathers, it gathers for a purpose; it gathers to do something. It's provocative, but you might call our approach to the Christian faith "make believe." Make. Believe. Make it real. Put it into practice. "Show me." Act like Jesus. Do what he did. Be his hands and heart right now, right here, in this world with its horrors and hungers and heartaches. What follows is something about the art of gathering and making believe.

GO DEEPER . . .

1. Remember an experience so powerful that it took your breath away. How do you keep the memory of it alive? How do you communicate its power to others?

2. What rituals have you participated in, past or present? How have those rituals affected you as an individual? As part of a group?

Chapter 2

Gathered for Hospitality

Have you ever heard the realtor's old advice for selling a house? When people come through to look at the place, make sure there's some bread baking in the oven.

While that might not be a practice you'll find in many churches on Sunday morning (although it is sometimes part of the service preparations at one church we know in Seattle), it is an example of a kind of hospitality we might want to think about—a subtle but powerful indication that we want you here and welcome your presence . . . even if it is to increase the chances that you'll buy this house.

We encounter hospitality in other everyday ways: the careful setting of a table at a good restaurant; the preparation that went into a worthwhile lecture; hours of chopping, cleaning and cooking before a neighborhood fiesta;

the often unnoticed labor of a hotel cleaning staff that leaves the guest room looking brand new.

Hospitality is powerful. The Bible describes it as one of the principal marks of the life and ministry of Jesus. His hospitality was profound—it went far beyond the polite details and provisions we tend to identify as hospitable in contemporary culture. In fact, Jesus's hospitality in the Scriptures flew in the face of the cultural expectations for his time. The conventionally religious were deeply offended by Jesus's practice of eating with all kinds of people, even and especially with those who were outside polite society. The Pharisees were typically known to complain, "He eats with sinners and tax collectors!" (Matthew 9:11).

And it wasn't just at dinner parties. The Bible stories are straightforward in showing Jesus receiving, talking with, and accepting things from people who would not ordinarily have been welcomed by a rabbi. He accepts the hospitality of women. He speaks with a despised Samaritan. In one case, after a fierce two-way conversation with a foreign woman about her daughter who was ill, Jesus admits that she has taught him something—that God's love is not limited

The Samaritans lived in what had been the northern kingdom of Israel. They accepted only the first five books of the Bible and worshiped the God of Israel. Their religion was not mainstream Judaism and they were looked down on by Jews. There is still a small community of Samaritans today, mostly in and around the city of Nablus in Israel.

to society's carefully drawn lines about who is acceptable and who is not (Matt. 15:22–28). Jesus does what genuinely hospitable people always do: He makes room for people to be who they are, just as they are, as God loves them.

Compassion: The Heart of Hospitality

Then again, Jesus's hospitality is not necessarily about conviviality or pleasant conversation or comfort. Some of his most hospitable acts likely made some people deeply *un*comfortable, like his presence at a dinner party thrown by a leader named Simon (Luke 7:36–50). Simon was hosting a formal meal, and the custom of the day was for guests to recline on couches, propped up on an elbow with their sandal-less feet tucked behind them. On this evening, a woman crashes the party, a woman who had a reputation as a "sinner" in the community. She has come to be close to Jesus, maybe to learn from him. Maybe she had already heard him teaching or witnessed a healing. In any case, she stands behind him and begins to weep. She has brought a jar of expensively perfumed oil (another version of the story says the ointment cost the equivalent of a year's wages) and in a lavish gesture she begins to weep and anoints Jesus's feet and wipes them with her hair.

It is not hard to image that Simon and his guests must have been shocked, not just at her actions, but that Jesus allows her to carry on like this. Jesus tells a story about a couple of people who owed some money, one a lot, the other not so much. The one who was owed the money for-gave both debts. Now which of the two debtors, asks Jesus, would be more grateful? Simon gives the obvious answer: the one whose debt was bigger. "Right," says Jesus. Then he turns to the woman and tells the room that what she is doing is a sign that her sins are forgiven.

The woman is exercising a kind of over-the-top act of hospitality that contrasts with Simon's failure to provide even the customary welcome of water to wash his guest's feet or oil to anoint his head. Because she offers so much love, Jesus stuns Simon and the other guests by announcing her sins are forgiven.

Jesus's kind of hospitality—whether he is extending it or receiving it—always begins to make real the compassion of God. Jesus tells his disciples, "Be merciful, as your Father is merciful" (Luke 6:36). A better translation of the word "merciful" might be "compassionate." "Be compassionate as God is compassionate."

To modern ears, the English word merciful might imply pity or even condescension. To show mercy can easily sug-gest feeling sorry for someone . . . from a certain distance. But the Hebrew and Aramaic word we translate as "**com-passion**" is the plural form of a noun that in its singular form means "womb." The word carries with it a sense of visceral empathy, a feeling-with—remember the word "pas-sion" comes from the Latin word meaning "to feel" and the prefix "com," "with"—as a mother for her children.

When Jesus welcomes people who are usually and sometimes profoundly unwelcome, he is making God's "wombish" love tangible and real.[1] Jesus's disciples and friends have been struggling to follow his command and example ever since.

Come Together

One of the primary ways we practice hospitality is to gather together. We learn to extend Jesus's kind of hospitality to others—to the stranger, the outcast, the unloved—by receiving that hospitality ourselves. When we come to a church service, we're really coming to a party, a celebration, a gathering focused on the love and mercy of God, who is the source of all life.

The authors of this book enjoy hosting dinner parties. In fact, we met and have developed our friendship in significant ways through our love of preparing and sharing good food. There is something primal and fundamentally human about sitting down together at table with family, friends and even strangers. Hospitality is an art form. It requires planning and preparation, effort and care. Even a simple or spontaneous invitation to come over for coffee or a chat seems to call for some forethought about how to welcome.

---

1. Robin Meyers, *Saving Jesus from the Church* (New York: HarperOne 2009), 126.

In churches, hospitality involves everything from who welcomes you at the door (or even in the parking lot) to signage (how easy is it to find the bathrooms?), the temperature of the room, the lighting, fragrances, sounds, arrangement of furniture, and the ways you are or are not invited and prepared to enter into the ritual or event.

This attention to preparation does not mean that it is the host's job to manage or control the guests. As anyone who offers hospitality in their home discovers, it is necessary to cultivate a willingness to accept people as they are. Any gathering of different people who come together to share food and drink and conversation can take on a life of its own—the host can never predict exactly what his or her guests will give or receive from interacting with one another.

While good hospitality does pay attention to helping guests feel comfortable at the gathering—that might include an explanation about the food being served, or how to use unfamiliar utensils, or simply introducing guests to one another—the point of setting people at ease is to allow them the freedom to express themselves and enjoy the company of others.

Shaping Raw Material

While at first glance worship in a typical Episcopal church may not look like there is a lot of room for personal expression, the hospitality that liturgy aims to provide is spacious enough to invite each person to bring his or her own experiences, convictions, questions, doubts, stories into relationship with those of other Christians through the ages. This is what makes the Christian tradition a living reality—one follower of Jesus handing on to another the experience of God's love and mercy. Scholar Jaroslav Pelikan once said it was important to make a distinction between the words "tradition" and "traditionalism." "Tradition," he said, "is the living faith of the dead, traditionalism is the dead faith of the living. And, I suppose I should add, it is traditionalism that gives tradition such a bad name."[2]

No two people will hear a text from the Bible exactly the same way, nor should we be expected to do so. Each person will experience and respond in his or her own way to a sermon or a prayer or a song or a visual image. What may comfort me in a given act of worship may disturb you. What you might find challenging one Sunday may seem like the best news there could be on another.

We each bring our own histories, experiences, life situations, expectations, hopes and dreams with us to church. What we encounter there will engage these realities, either welcoming them or signaling that they are unwelcome and might better be left at the door. If they are welcomed, if we are made to feel we are welcomed just as we are, then the experience of God's hospitality will be shaped by the very people

2. Jaroslav Pelikan, "Tradition as Heritage: A Vindication," in *The Vindication of Tradition: The 1983 Jefferson Lecture in the Humanities* (New Haven, CT: Yale University Press, 1984), 65–82. Retrieved from http://www.jstor.org/stable/j.ctt5hk0sg.7.

The **Didache** is "The Teaching of the Twelve Apostles" and scholars date it to the early second century.

who gather. Our lives become the raw material for the liturgical experience—the people who gather are the means by which God is present.

The ancient Christian conviction is that when we gather in the name of Jesus Christ, God is present. Jesus said, "For where two or three are gathered in my name, I am there among them" (Matt. 18:20). One of the earliest texts we have describing aspects of Christian worship, a document known as the *Didache,* points to the same conviction. A line from it has been paraphrased into a hymn sung in many Episcopal churches:

> As grain, once scattered on the hillsides
> was in this broken bread made one,
> so from all lands thy Church be gathered
> into thy kingdom by thy Son."[3]

Sacramental Hospitality

Here we should take note of another ancient Christian conviction, namely, that it is baptism that incorporates new members into the Body of Christ. This washing in water signifies the fullness of the church's hospitality to those who

---

3. "Father, We Thank Thee Who Hast Planted," *The Hymnal 1982* (New York: Church Hymnal, 1985), hymn 302.

are coming to faith in Christ. In the early centuries of the Christian movement there developed a lengthy and lavish process of welcoming new Christians into the community of faith called the **catechumenate.** It involved a series of public prayers for those who were preparing for baptism, who were learning to live more and more like Jesus, and being invited step-by-step into greater commitment to the Christian way of life.

> The word "**catechumenate**" comes from a Greek word meaning "to echo the teaching." The catechumenate has been restored to the Episcopal Church in a companion volume to the Book of Common Prayer called *The Book of Occasional Services.*

Converts to the faith were led gradually to the water of baptism, accompanied by sponsors and the whole community. They did not receive communion until their baptism. In fact, sharing in the bread and wine of the Eucharist was seen as the culmination of baptism, and every Eucharist thereafter was a participation in the mystery of their incorporation into the Body of Christ. The Episcopal Church officially maintains the historic relationship between baptism and communion. The **canons** of the church insist that people should be baptized before they may receive communion.

However, in many Episcopal churches today, there is an intentional invitation to

> **Canons** are various rules that the church adopts to govern its common life. They might be thought of as guard rails to keep members of the church from running off the road.

everyone to receive the bread and wine of the Eucharist, baptized or not. There is a lively debate among Episcopalians and other Christians about the appropriateness of this open invitation. Many people are convinced that one of the principle marks of the ministry of Jesus was his radically inclusive table fellowship, and so for Christians who follow his example, any prerequisite or barrier to the Lord's table makes no sense. Others cite the ancient practice of coming to participation in the Eucharist through baptism as making sacramental sense, that the Eucharist is "not just any meal" and that an overly casual approach to it does inadequate justice to it and to those receiving communion. The debate continues.

The authors of this book want to enter this conversation through the doorway of hospitality. In the parish in Seattle where we served together several years ago, there was careful attention to the welcoming of people who were new to the Christian faith. We practiced a version of the ancient catechumenate. Newcomers to the faith gathered every week to reflect on their lives in the light of the Bible's stories about God's actions in human life and the definitive entrance of God into this world in the life, death, and resurrection of Jesus. Every week, these people, preparing for their own baptisms, were prayed for and blessed publicly at the main service.

In the ancient catechumenate, those preparing for baptism were dismissed from the assembly after the sermon; they were sent out to continue their formation before the prayer over the bread and wine and communion. One year, our catechumens were particularly intrigued by this practice and asked if we might adopt it in our own congregation. So that Lent, after the sermon, the deacon sent them out to go with their sponsors to "feast on the word of God."

One young woman in particular had been really interested in taking on this practice and after her baptism that Easter we asked her what her experience had been like. She said, "I've never felt so honored in my life. The whole church stood there praying for us as we went out to dive deeper into the Bible and our lives." She had experienced the dismissal before communion as an act of profound hospitality. "Everyone was taking us so seriously," she said.

Another young man, a computer software developer with no religious background at all, had come to our church at the invitation of a friend and discovered a deep longing to follow Jesus. After being prepared for his baptism this way, we asked him what the most meaningful thing had been on his journey to the font. He said, "I've never been touched like that." What? "Yeah," he said, "I've never felt cared for quite like that." He was referring to the way his sponsor and teachers prayed for him and the others at the end of every Bible study session. They prayed for each person individually, making the sign of the cross on their foreheads.

We wonder what it would be like if these kinds of experiences were more typical in our congregations, if this kind of careful, even lavish ritual hospitality were the norm and the standard of our welcome for those who are drawn to the Christian faith. What would we be communicating to both the casual visitor and the long-standing member?

• • •

The hospitality of God is true. God will not be satisfied until every man, woman, and child knows that they have a welcome place at the table of God's love. The life of the church is one lengthy response to the mystery of God's love, a response that longs to make real what is already true. Our response is worthy of the best we can offer.

GO DEEPER . . .

1. What is the most memorable act of hospitality you've experienced?

2. Have you ever entered a church and felt truly welcome? Have you entered a church and felt a lack of hospitality? Recall the story of what happened in each instance.

Chapter 3

Gathered around the Story

"That's one small step for man; one giant leap for mankind."
I (Dent) remember it like it was yesterday. Our family had
gathered at our grandparents' cabin outside the town of
Bremerton, Washington. It was a beautiful July day in 1969.
The waters of Puget Sound were sparkling in the sunlight,
and the aroma of my grandfather's lemon garlic chicken
wafted from the rotisserie grill on the deck.

But on that warm summer day, we were all inside, eyes
fixed on the old black-and-white TV set, topped with "rab-
bit ears" for optimal reception. Walter Cronkite narrated the
whole event, and I remember feeling like I was a part of
history, just by watching and hearing.

After Armstrong's walk and memorable words, my
grandfather looked at me and my brother John, and with

a twinkle in his eye, he said, "You know, I've built my own rocket ship and hidden it in the woods behind the property here. Why don't you boys go out and see if you can find it, and while you're at it, pick lots of blackberries!" He had spun this yarn before, claiming that he had also placed his rocket in plain view at Boeing Field in Seattle, in the form of a green airplane fuselage that we later learned was a flight simulator. But that didn't matter. We wanted Grandpa Jack to tell his stories as often as possible.

That cabin on Puget Sound was a mystical, magical story place, a place where history enveloped us, and memories were made. As the relentless, quiet tick tock of the mantel clock ran on, so did the stories.

Storytelling was always a part of the way we came together as a family. And it was always Thanksgiving that crowned the year with tales. On the sideboard there was a crock of creamed onions, a recipe of my dearly departed great grandmother (affectionately named "Goggy"). Every year Goggy's creamed onions sat on the sideboard, barely touched by anyone. Invariably, conversation would turn to the savory dish, and to the hands that had once lovingly prepared it. "Who's making Goggy's creamed onions next year?" one of us would ask, giggling. And everyone around the table followed suit with laughter, and a sweet remembering of that dear woman.

All of these stories gave me a sense of the noble, adventurous, hard-edged and gentle lineage that had gone before me—a venerable history to which I am an heir and participant. You may have a similar tradition of sharing your family history at your table or at tables full of old friends. Stop and think for a moment: How did those stories touch you and shape the person you are today? How are you retelling those stories?

Making Dry Bones Live

Gathering family and friends at Thanksgiving is very much like gathering to celebrate the Eucharist. Once we have greeted friends and family from far and wide and welcomed them into the home, stories come naturally. They can be as simple as catching up on recent details of our daily lives. More often than not, they begin to reflect the past—our collective history.

It is much the same when we gather to worship. Week in and week out we hear and respond to the **lectionary.** Imagine the potential effect around the world as millions of people hear the gospel story of the Sermon on the Mount, or Jesus's encounter with the Samaritan woman at the well, or countless other stories. What if we allowed these passages to do deep work in us, renewing our sense of purpose as ministers, so that we might then go into our communities and show others what change looks like?

If told well, these stories have the power to capture our imagination, to form and transform us. Every time we retell the story of creation from Gen-

The **lectionary** is the collection of Scripture readings that many Christians around the world hear on a given Sunday or in a given week.

esis, we have the opportunity to think about the great void. The nothingness. "In the beginning, God . . . ." Only God. How do we wrap our limited minds around such a concept? As the story unfolds, the Spirit of God sweeps across the face of the waters. Light. Darkness. Sun, moon and stars; land, seas, mountains and valleys. Green growing things, and creatures too many to number. The creator takes what was chaos, and shapes it into exquisite order, an order of which each of us is a part. It is a cosmic, mystical answer to the question: "Where do I come from, and why am I here?" And we begin to realize our connectedness to God, who called us into being, fashioning us in the divine image.

All too soon, we hear Old Testament stories of how we reject the beauty of this created order by a willful action that leads us to separation from God. As the story moves forward, we hear of God's desperate yearning to bring us back into relationship, over and over again.

The Great Vigil and the Great Story

At our church in Seattle, the yearly liturgical planning time took place in the late summer. Beginning with the **Great Vigil of Easter**, we would revisit the stories and the accom-

The Great Vigil of Easter is a lengthy and lavish celebration of the mystery of Jesus's death and resurrection. It is usually held after sundown on the Holy Saturday before Easter or before sunrise on Easter Sunday. Traditionally, baptisms occur at the Vigil.

panying responses, prayers and actions, culminating in the waters of baptism, making new Christians, and the joy of proclaiming Easter once again. Then we let that energy bubble over and flow out over the rest of the year's planning.

The Vigil is the quintessential model for every Sunday celebration, marked by gathering in the dark, striking the new fire, following the light into the church, and then hearing and responding to the ancient stories, which are also *our* stories. These are stories of promise and hope for a people who lived thousands of years ago, and for a people gathered around the same stories today.

One of those stories tells of the prophet Ezekiel (chapter 37) being mystically led by the Spirit of God into a valley filled with dry bones—a metaphor for the whole house of Israel, who had lost hope. The Spirit tells Ezekiel to prophesy to the bones: to come together, take on flesh and stand up. But there is one thing lacking: breath. The Spirit comes from the four winds, bringing God's own breath to fill the house of Israel with new life and hope. How does the church get its dry, dry bones put back together, enfleshed, and filled with the breath of God in everyday life? God says, "I will be your God, and I will be with you." When we gather around these stories, we, like the dry bones, become God's own people.

Stories like this are rich nourishment for a hungry people. For this reason, we believe the word should be proclaimed with an appropriate sense of drama and context. When we train readers, we should remind them these are the most important words they will speak this week. These are stories about people who encountered the Living God, whose lives and futures were indelibly transformed. Why should those stories not have the same impact now? Instead of seeing the Bible as a "how-to" book, we like to think of it as a "why-to" book. It leads us to risk stepping into unknown territory, only to find it might be a giant leap into possibility.

In his memoir, *Auntie Mame: An Irreverent Escapade*, author Patrick Dennis quotes his irascible aunt as saying something like, "Life's a banquet, and most poor suckers are starving to death!"[1] Unfortunately, I have visited churches in which the proclamation of Scripture did not seem very much like a banquet. If the readings are half-rehearsed, or mumbled, or rushed through nervously, who could blame people for being disinterested or unmoved?

Stories Push Us out the Door

The stories in Scripture tell how God's people took bold steps into a new life. In the same manner, these stories give us hope and courage to take giant leaps in being the church, God's living presence in the world.

For instance, in Exodus 3, Moses encounters God in the form of a burning bush. After considerable arguing, God prevails upon Moses to head back into Egypt to help God

---

1. Patrick Dennis, *Auntie Mame: An Irreverent Escapade* (New York: Broadway Books, 1955), 298.

set the people free. God hears their cry in bondage and wants to act in human history to liberate them, so Moses answers: "Yes." By doing so, he is transformed into a true leader, one who helps to describe the relationship between God and God's people. Why do we read this story at least once a year? We can mirror God's deep desire for our liberation by living our lives in ways that set our own sisters and brothers free. Our "yes" is the same as Moses's "yes" to God. Moses's small step into the parted Red Sea is a giant leap for God's people into freedom.

In John 11, Martha and Mary are crushed with grief over the death of their brother, Lazarus. They send for Jesus, who intentionally comes too late to their town. The story tells us he is visibly moved at Lazarus's tomb, so moved that with tear-filled eyes, he commands Lazarus to come forth. And when the revived figure steps out of the tomb, he tells the community, "Unbind him, and let him go." Those few small steps for a once-dead man become a giant leap for the people of God: calling them and us to be liberators.

We can also look to John 20. After the crucifixion, the young church gathers in fear, locking themselves away to hide. When Jesus sends the Spirit, a fresh boldness overtakes them, leading them to go out and tell the stories of Jesus far and wide. In doing so, they become part of the story, performing their own miracles in shared community, caring for one another, healing and feeding one another, speaking truth to worldly power and witnessing to a power far greater than any state or religious structure: the power of God's love.

Thinking about God's "kindom" instead of God's "kingdom" invites people to recognize the mutual dependence of creation rather than humans' dominion over it.

Every Christian is not only an heir to this history, but also a part of the continuing story of God's plan of salvation in the world and of the ongoing unfolding of God's Kindom on earth. Our stories push us toward sharing the eucharistic feast at hand and becoming the body of Christ. They feed us and push us out the door to proclaim the good news in our words and in our actions.

When we take a few small steps out beyond our big red doors, carrying the word of God with us, giant leaps become possible in our families, in our communities, and in the world.

GO DEEPER . . .

1. Think of the stories of your own life (if you've got time, create a timeline of the major moments that shaped your life). Which ones stand out as powerful or poignant? How do you share or reflect on them today?

2. What stories from Scripture resonate with your own experience or the experience of communities of which you are part?

Chapter 4

Gathered for Offering

And here we offer and present unto thee,
O Lord, our selves, our souls and bodies,
to be a reasonable, holy, and living sacrifice
unto thee . . .

These words appeared in the very first edition of the Book of Common Prayer in 1549, and you can still hear them in Episcopal churches that offer **Rite I** celebrations of the Eucharist. Prayers of offering represent an impulse that seems to come from deep within the human condition. Throughout time and within many cultural contexts human beings have been drawn to make offerings to God or to the gods. They offer the first fruits of the harvest to ensure a productive growing season. Animals are slaughtered to placate an angry or righteous God. Money and

"Rite I" refers to one of the forms provided in the prayer book that preserves much of the Elizabethan language of earlier versions of the Book of Common Prayer.

other forms of material wealth are brought and offered in the service of God.

It is common to call these kinds of offerings "sacrifices." But we might need to consider the word sacrifice in its specifically Christian context. The word **sacrifice** simply means "to make holy." While there are several different kinds of sacrifices described in the Hebrew Scriptures—often aimed at different religious purposes—they all have their origin in making possible a sacred meal, "sealing the deal," so to speak, confirming or repairing the agreement or covenant between God and humankind.

Sacrifice and Covenant

When I (Jeff) visited our companion diocese in what is now the country of South Sudan, our caravan of four wheelers, after many hours of driving, was met outside a small village in the countryside with singing and dancing. We were there to dedicate a new church building, a small structure called a *tukal*. As we walked toward the place to be dedicated, I noticed a large white object in the path ahead of us. As we got closer, the object turned out to be a large white cow, its legs tied together while it lay on its side. As we got even closer, suddenly someone stepped up to the cow and deftly slit its throat.

My companions and I were invited to step over the now dying animal as a kind of startlingly traditional and lavish gesture of welcome. The whole village feasted that evening in celebration of our visit, a ritually significant meal to honor our solidarity, the life and faith shared between friends in Sudan and North America.

In Genesis 15 there is a mysterious story about a sacrifice offered by Abraham. In essence, what it describes might not be so different from the offering of that cow in a South Sudanese village. God instructs Abraham to find and kill a heifer, a ram, a goat, a dove, and a pigeon and then cut them in half (except the birds) and lay them in pieces in two rows with a path between them. Night comes and God appears in the form of a "smoking fire pot and a flaming torch." As Abraham falls into a deep and troubled sleep, the text says, the fire pot and the torch pass between the pieces of the sacrifice.

The origins of this story might well refer to ancient Near Eastern agreements about land treaties, where each party would pass through the slaughtered animals as if to say, "May this happen to me if I break this deal." In this case, it is God alone who passes through the slaughtered animals. This is God reiterating the promise to Abraham that God will make this man's descendants God's own people. And the only party who counts in this covenant agreement is God. The promise is God's. It does not depend on Abraham, so Abraham and his descendants can rely on all the promises God makes. The sacrifice is a kind of ritual meal, an offering to God as the other party in the feast.

Much of the Hebrew Scriptures are filled with descriptions of various kinds of sacrifices—either how to perform them and under what circumstances—or prophets criticizing Israel for keeping the sacrifices correctly but without the necessary change of heart or disposition they are meant to signify.

> When the prophet Micah wonders what more besides the formal rituals the people of Israel could do to be in God's favor, the answer comes, "He has told you, O mortal, what is good; and what does the LORD require of you but to do justice, and to love kindness, and to walk humbly with your God?" (Mic. 6:8)

The Feast of Passover was the centerpiece of the whole sacrificial tradition in Israel. It commemorated the exodus of the Hebrew people from their slavery in Egypt. The book of Exodus tells of a series of plagues sent by God to convince Pharaoh to release the Hebrew slaves. One after another they fail to convince him until the most terrible plague of all is sent. The angel of death kills all the first-born children of the Egyptians.

The Hebrews avoid this terror by killing a lamb, one for each household or shared between smaller households, and then smearing some of its blood on the doorposts of their houses so the angel of death will pass them by and spare them. The lamb is eaten in a hastily prepared meal with unleavened bread, because there is no time even to allow it to rise. Pharaoh sends the slaves packing, and so begins the story of Israel at the Red Sea, the forty years of wilderness wandering and the Ten Commandments. Together, these make up the story of Israel discovering itself as the people of God. For faithful Jews, the sacrificial meal of Passover is the yearly reminder of this identity.

Christ Our Passover Is Sacrificed

The death and resurrection of Jesus took place at the time of Passover. The powerful images and themes of Passover were in the air as the events of Jesus's last days in the flesh unfolded. It is quite understandable that Jesus's first friends, who were observant Jews after all, came quickly to make sense of the meaning of his death and resurrection in terms of a sacrifice. Eventually, the first Christians came to understand the death and resurrection of Jesus as the **Paschal Mystery,** the culmination or fulfillment of the whole sacrificial system.

In the account of the crucifixion in John 19, when Jesus breathes his last, the curtain in the temple separating the Holy of Holies (the holy space where the fullness of God's presence was thought to dwell) from the rest of the temple is torn in two from top to bottom. In other words, God did it. Before, only the high priest could enter the Holy of Holies with sacrificial blood; now, the gospel seems to say, the way to holiness has been opened to all by God through the cross.

> *Pascha* is simply a Greek version of the Hebrew *Pesach*, Passover. Many European languages use it for what we call Easter in English— *Pasqua* in Italian, *Pacques* in French. In other words, Easter is the Christian Passover.

If you have been to an Episcopal church, this story may sound vaguely familiar. In the celebration of the Eucharist, after the priest breaks the bread, there is a brief silence and then she says or sings, "Alleluia, Christ our Passover is sacrificed for us." The people respond, "Therefore let us keep the feast. Alleluia." This self-offering of God is made present to us and for us in the sharing of this meal. Notice the present tense. The words of the liturgy do not say, "Christ was sacrificed for us some two thousand years ago. Let's all remember it fondly." No, the words declare that the sacrifice of Christ is happening right now in our midst.

In many Episcopal churches the bread and wine of the Eucharist are lifted up at the conclusion of the **Great Thanksgiving** , and the deacon and priest may make a gesture of reverence (like bowing) before the bread and cup. It is not uncommon to see people reverence in the same way as they leave their seats to come to receive the bread and wine. These gestures are an expression of our conviction that the Risen Christ is actually present with us in these gifts.

On the whole, Episcopalians have resisted the temptation to insist on theological explanations for how this is so. Our primary theology is expressed by the words and actions of our liturgical celebrations themselves. And what those words and actions reveal is the church's ancient faith that not only is the Risen Jesus present in the bread and wine, but also present in those who gather

The Greek word *eucharstia* simply means "thanksgiving." That is why the lengthy prayer over the bread and wine is called the **Great Thanksgiving** to keep this feast. We can hold up the bread of the Eucharist and declare it to be the Body of Christ, because we are already the Body of Christ. St. Augustine, who was born in the year 354, made the same point when he wrote of the bread, "Become what you see, and receive what you are." In other words, you really are what you eat.

Rooted in Grace

We have already spoken of the importance of making believe—that is, acting in such a way that the faith we profess is made real in the world. One such belief is in the grace of God. The love and mercy of God no longer depend on a system of sacrifices that we offer to God. Rather, in the vulnerability of Jesus on the cross, God offers to *us*. Still, it is common for Christians to talk about making offerings to God. In the Prayers of the People we offer our intercessions, our requests, our longings, our concerns to God. In that moment called the Peace, when we turn to one another and offer each other a sign of Christ's peace—whether with a simple handshake or a more exuberant embrace—in a real sense we are ritually opening and offering ourselves to one another.

> There are several set forms for the Prayers of the People in the Book of Common Prayer. In the contemporary language of Rite II, those forms are intended as models for congregations to compose their own prayers in response to their own contexts.

The Book of Common Prayer talks about the collection and presentation of gifts of money and bread and wine at the Eucharist as the Offertory; some churches also gather food and other provisions for those in need in the same moment. In one of the prayers said over the bread and wine, the priest says, "We celebrate the memorial of our redemption . . . in this sacrifice of praise and thanksgiving . . . and we offer you these gifts." The Eucharist is a sacrifice, an offering of praise. We do not offer our prayers or our presence or our money or the bread and wine on the altar in hopes that God will take notice and look on us with favor. God has already accepted us. God loves us more than we can comprehend. God has decided to love us despite our sinfulness, despite our breaking of the covenant. And so every offering we make is an act of pure, astonished thanksgiving.

GO DEEPER . . .

1. How do you understand the word "sacrifice"? Have you ever made a sacrifice for someone else? Has anyone ever sacrificed for you? What occurred as a result of either of these acts?

2. The next time you're in a church, notice the moments related to offering and sacrifice. What stands out?

Chapter 5

Gathered
to Be Sent

The Church is most truly itself, the Body of
Christ, when it lives and breathes mission.
The heart of this body is mission—both
domestic and foreign mission—in partnership
with anyone who shares that passion. Indeed,
our baptismal identity is grounded in commitment to mission and in the assurance that
in our faithful pursuit of that mission God will
bless both us and our work.

—The Most Reverend Katharine Jefferts Schori,
26th Presiding Bishop and
Primate of the Episcopal Church

We spoke of hospitality in the early chapters of this book.
It welcomes and invites people to encounter the dying and
risen Christ in the context of community. That journey
begins with gathering. As the sacred story unfolds, we find
deeper meaning and confirm our identity as God's own
people. As we offer prayer and our very selves in bread and
wine, in money and music, we reflect the self-giving Love

Mission derives from the Latin word *missio*, which means "sent."

of Jesus, the Christ. As we celebrate this holy meal, we literally taste and see that God is good. In this high giving of thanks, we share a foretaste of the heavenly banquet. This inexorable rhythm nourishes us. It forms and transforms us. When we worship like we mean it, we are motivated, equipped, empowered to take the next step— the step toward **mission**. Our current presiding bishop, the Most Reverend Michael Curry, is known for his bold sending prayers. In one sermon, he urged people:

> Go share the Good News that we've just shared.
> Go be the face and hands and feet and heart of God
>   in the world.
> Go change the world—turn it upside down!

He usually goes on to explain that when we go out to turn the world upside down, we are actually putting it right side up, that is, back to God's original and eternal purpose for relationship with all of Creation. But all that work begins with being sent.

Time to Go

Some years ago, members of the Ministries Team in the Diocese of Chicago created a program of community learning focused on congregational vitality at every imaginable level. We called the program Thrive. In the pilot year, we invited about twenty congregations to make a serious two-year commitment to monthly Saturday learning sessions, with two overnight retreats together. Each congregation sent a rector or vicar (the lead priest in the church) and three to four lay leaders to be the Thrive Team, with an accountability team back home to help disseminate the information and keep participating congregations up to date.

We created a curriculum that took groups on a deep dive into crucial topics like community identity, leadership theory, conflict management and resolution, stewardship, and hospitality. Sessions began and ended with worship and song. We invited the teams to share learnings and insights at round table discussions and to engage with art and drama to take the learning deeper.

The Thrive Session focused on Sunday morning liturgy was particularly powerful. Part of our work/play was to identify "liturgical sacred cows," those elements that may have little or no meaning in twenty-first century worship, but no one dares to mess with. People were invited to inscribe the sacred cows on paper and then launch them on the "cattlepult." One by one, sacred cows went flying—our collective, symbolic letting go.

We also asked provocative discussion questions like: "Why sing?" and "Why worship?" and "What do we think we are doing on Sunday mornings?" But none got more attention than this intentional set-up question: "What if we moved coffee hour from after the service to *before* the service?"

The gasps in the room indicated we had landed at one of the most sacred of all cows. Why? In most churches, the deacon dismisses the people at the end of the liturgy with words like these: "Go forth in the name of Christ." "Go in peace to love and serve the Lord." "Let us go forth into the world rejoicing in the power of the Spirit."

Those words cue several predictable reactions. Some congregations sit and listen to a well-practiced postlude, perhaps applauding politely at the end. Some kneel reverently for a final moment of personal prayer before departing, often watching and waiting until the very last candle is extinguished. Others carry on in raucous conversation and laughter as they head to coffee hour. Often meetings are scheduled after worship. The list goes on and on.

But how many take the words of the deacon seriously and "Go!" These are not mild suggestions. They are marching orders. Having gathered and feasted on word, prayer, and sacrament, we are prepared to be God's people in the world. This one hour of worship could be like a sling-shot, hurtling us into the remaining 167 hours of the week outside the walls of the church. We go forth, each of us in our own unique way, to share God's love in a world that aches and hungers for a taste of that love.

In a sense, passing through the doors from the church building into the world is akin to a birth. We emerge formed and transformed, a Church birthed in water and fire. The liturgy is designed to motivate and send us out to take on the risky, passionate work of the Gospel. In chapter 7 on baptism, you will see what we call the "So-What Questions." The liturgy sends us to enact and embody our answers to those questions.

Episcopalians say the **Jesus Movement** is the ongoing community of people who follow Jesus into loving, liberating, life-giving relationship with God, each other, and creation.

As we go about that work, we are constantly drawn back to the community, to gather again and retell our stories, to pray and celebrate and feast—only to be sent out again. We repeat a holy rhythm that perpetually reminds us that we are to show the world around us how to die and rise, and die and rise again. This is the pulse or rhythm of what Jesus calls the Church. These days, we also understand it as the **Jesus Movement**.[1]

While only a few of our Thrive Teams actually took this pre-liturgy coffee hour idea to their congregations, one team came up with a great compromise of sorts. Instead of calling it coffee hour, they decided to call it mission strategy hour. The idea was to share hospitality and conversation, while becoming more intentionally mission-minded—a very creative solution that reminded people that mission, or being sent, is the whole point of our worship.

---

1. Learn more about the Jesus Movement in Michael Curry's *Following the Way of Jesus,* volume 7 of the Church's Teachings for a Changing World series (New York: Church Publishing, 2017).

Going Forth like We Mean It

As a musician and liturgist, I (Dent) notice how many of the songs and Scriptures we sing and read inside the church are actually designed to send us out. Already we have remarked on the hymn drawn from the ancient *Didache*:

> As grain, once scattered on the hillsides
> was in this broken bread made one,
> so from all lands thy Church be gathered
> into thy kingdom by thy Son.[2]

Once scattered, we are gathered into the kingdom. Is this a divine script for gathering up of all God's people at the end of the age, or might it describe the rhythm of the church? Perhaps it is both. We are gathered in at the beginning of the liturgy. We are broken open and poured out in the celebration of the Eucharist. Finally we are sent out, scattered again to be the kingdom, to live out God's reign in all its glory and messiness, its joy and pain.

The truth is, "Go!" might well be the operative word for the church in all times and places. Sending is a part of God's plan from way back:

> Go down, Moses, way down in Egypt's land.
> Tell old Pharaoh to let my people go.[3]

---

2. "Father, We Thank Thee Who Hast Planted," *The Hymnal 1982,* hymn 302.

3. "When Israel Was in Egypt's Land," *The Hymnal 1982,* hymn 648.

Moses's mission was to make God known and to liberate God's people from slavery. They needed to be free so they could go and participate in blessing and freeing other oppressed people, in the name of God.

That same calling echoes through the pages of the Bible and throughout the liturgy. Here is only a sampling:

"The reaper is already receiving wages and is gathering fruit for eternal life, so that sower and reaper may rejoice together. For here the saying holds true, 'One sows and another reaps.' I sent you to reap that for which you did not labor. Others have labored, and you have entered into their labor."

John 4:36–38

Jesus said to them again, "Peace be with you. As the Father has sent me, so I send you."

John 20:21

"As you have sent me into the world, so I have sent them into the world."

John 17:18

"But you will receive power when the Holy Spirit has come upon you; and you will be my witnesses in Jerusalem, in all Judea and Samaria, and to the ends of the earth."

Acts 1:8

"Go therefore and make disciples of all the nations, baptizing them in the name of the Father and the Son and the Holy Spirit, teaching them to observe all that I commanded you. And remember, I am with you always, to the end of the age."

Matthew 28:19–20

[A]nd he sent them out to proclaim the kingdom of God and to heal.

Luke 9:2

And He said to them, "Go into all the world and proclaim the good news to the whole creation."

Mark 16:15

"[B]ut go rather to the lost sheep of the house of Israel."

Matthew 10:6

It's unmistakably clear: We are gathered to be sent.

Several deacons I know dismiss their respective congregations with roughly these words: "The liturgy is ended, let the service begin." In other words, the reign of Christ depends on us now. We go forth like we mean it, as people who have an impact on the world around us. We are not called to go meekly on our way; we are called to go out in bold confidence that we are God's own people, equipped and sent to do "greater works than these" as Jesus promises in John 14:12.

"It is not that God's church has a mission, but that God's mission has a church." —*Archbishop of Canterbury Rowan Williams*

Presenting Ourselves Back to God

As a chorister at Christ Church Cathedral in Victoria, British Columbia, I (Dent) sang an anthem well known to many singers: "Greater Love Hath No Man," by English composer John Ireland. The scriptural texts for this anthem have stuck with me ever since I was eleven years old:

> Ye are washed, ye are sanctified, ye are justified in the name of the Lord Jesus. Ye are a chosen generation, a royal priesthood, a holy nation. That ye should show forth the praises of him who hath call'd you out of darkness into his marvellous light. I beseech your brethren, by the mercies of God, that ye present your bodies, a living sacrifice, holy and acceptable unto God, which is your reasonable service.

Even typing those words I can feel the energizing charge coming from the first lines, and then the calm response as we present ourselves back to God, our reasonable service. We present ourselves in the world, as if to say, "I go."

This is the whole point of gathering to celebrate the Eucharist: to become "living members of the Living Christ"[4] in and among the world. Imagine if we sang this hymn with conviction:

---

4. "We Know That Christ is Raised and Dies No More," *The Hymnal 1982,* hymn 296.

We have no mission but to serve in full obedience to our
   Lord:
to care for all without reserve and spread Christ's liberating word.[5]

Sharing the stories, making offering, gathering with
compassion, meditating on texts like this—all these elements eventually send us out into the world emboldened,
empowered, with renewed energy to take risks and act with
audacious love.

GO DEEPER . . .

1. Next time you're in church, look at the mission statement (you may find it on the website
   or in the worship bulletin). How does the
   mission statement match up with what you
   experience and hear in worship?

2. How do you understand your own place in
   God's mission? Is there anything you believe
   God is sending you in the world to be or to
   do?

---

5. "The Church of Christ in Every Age," *Wonder, Love, and Praise: A
Supplement to the Hymnal 1982* (New York: Church Publishing, 1997),
hymn 779.

Chapter 6

Gathered to Sing

God is our Song, and every singer blest
Who, praising him, finds energy and rest.
All who praise God with unaffected joy
Give back to us the wisdom we destroy.

God is our Song, for Jesus comes to save;
While praising him we offer all we have.
New songs we sing, in ventures new unite,
When Jesus leads us upward into light.

This is the Song no conflict ever drowns;
Who praises God all human wrath disowns.
Love knows what rich complexities of sound
God builds upon a simple, common ground.

God is our Silence when no songs are sung,
When ecstasy or sorrow stills the tongue.
Glorious the faith which silently obeys
Until we find again the voice of praise.[1]

---

1. Fred Pratt Green, Hope Publishing Company, 1976.

I (Dent) have sung this text since I was in my late teens. Fred Pratt Green's poem is a profound expression of the power of song to transform the singer. This great gift of God, like most gifts, is meant to be shared. It is an intimate part of relationship with God, with the self, and with the community. Words alone can take us to certain depths and heights, but words sung can take us far deeper and higher and much further than we can otherwise imagine.

The Power of Song

Think of your favorite hymn or chorus, or of an old favorite that the whole congregation just belts out. It can be truly thrilling to sing in the midst of other people. Or consider how monastic communities chant with an intuitive quality that can only come with singing all 150 psalms each month. Rich tones ring forth in chant melodies, both simple and complex. The tradition of **call-and-response**—common among communities that don't rely on written music, but instead on aural teaching—is not only about the song; it is about a deep communication between caller and responder(s). Such music fundamentally rallies people together, in worship, in prayer, and in protest. Often repetitive, it is designed to use the ear rather than rely on reading notes on paper, and lends itself well to improvisation.

Call-and-response singing has found new life in Episcopal churches via a style known as "paperless music."

Singing does something to us that goes beyond a physical act. Making music with our bodies in community disarms and excites. Endorphins are released, joy bubbles up. Tears may even flow. It can unlock feelings, or express what we may have thought was inexpressible.

When I was in fifth grade, my teacher, Mrs. Chadwick, taught us key concepts by singing them: times tables, parts of speech, even the list of birds native to the Pacific Northwest. I imagine all or most of my classmates were able to retain that information because we sang it. The same holds true for liturgy and theology. Often we know the words of hymns by heart. Think of any Christmas carol, and you will soon find that you have a little (or large) theological library in your brain, because you downloaded it via singing. That is the magic of song. When we sing words we learn them in a different way than we do reading or hearing them.

An old song can trigger all sorts of feelings. Studies suggest that music, song especially, also links powerfully to memory. Dementia patients who had been unable to express themselves in speech can be liberated when invited to join in a familiar song like "Amazing Grace." That grace is truly amazing when someone who has been lost in a haze suddenly lights up and joins in the song.

Perfect Praise

When visiting congregations I ask people to have conversation about what song does to and for them. Many people say it has unifying power. It is expressive, it energizes, and to some it is terrifying. Singing is a very intimate act, and it contains an element of risk for some, who may feel almost naked when they sing.

I often ask, "How many of you were told as a child not to sing?" Usually the hands of about half the crowd go up, some of them very quickly. "I can't carry a tune in a bucket." Another person once exclaimed, "My wife says I sound like a buzz saw." Often people share these confessions with a smile on their faces, as if it is humorous. Others are more reticent to raise their hands, perhaps because they accepted and believed the words of so-called teachers and still bear the shame and trauma. The truth is, it requires a good deal of retraining, pastoral care, encouragement and essentially writing "permission slips" to coax people out of their insecurity about singing.

I have witnessed people breaking down in cleansing tears, because they were finally allowed to sing. St. Augustine famously reminds us that "those who sing pray twice," and often people who are able to access this special kind of prayer for the first time experience something of a spiritual breakthrough. A whole new world opens up.

It is unfortunate that so many people cling to the belief that any musical offering must be flawless. It is God who perfects our praises, as the prayer book reminds us:

O God, whom saints and angels delight to worship in heaven: Be ever present with your servants who seek through art and music to perfect the praises offered by

your people on earth; and grant to them even now
glimpses of your beauty, and make them worthy at
length to behold it unveiled for evermore; through Jesus
Christ our Lord. Amen.[2]

While this collect has a nobility and loveliness about it, I
think it presents a potential problem. Some musicians take
the verb "perfect" too seriously, as if it is their sole objec-
tive or obligation to make things perfect, and to be the sole
arbiter of taste in musical selections.

I used to be "that" organist/choirmaster. I rigidly adhered
to a set of expectations that allowed for music from the offi-
cial Episcopal hymnals and rarely from any other approved
resource, and certainly nothing that had not been deemed an
"approved resource." Likewise, choral music came exclu-
sively from the Anglican choral tradition, augmented by
respected and accepted American composers.

In God's own mysterious way, it was revealed to me that
I was not serving God's mission or my congregation, but
rather myself. I began the careful work of expanding the
musical menu for worship in the congregations I served.
To be sure, music from the classical Anglican tradition is
included. We now also include global music, gospel and
jazz, paperless or call-and-response music. I also encourage
both choir and congregation to let go, to improvise harmo-

---

2. "For Church Musicians and Artists," *The Book of Common Prayer*
(Church Hymnal, 1979), 819.

nies and to sing what they feel. The result is stunning, and it gets to the heart of what it means to make believe. We deeply learn what we sing.

As a result, I prefer sharing the following Choristers' Prayer with groups in my care. It comes from the Royal School of Church Music:

> Bless, O Lord, us your servants who minister in your Temple. Grant that what we sing with our lips we may believe in our hearts. And what we believe in our hearts we may show forth in our lives. Through Jesus Christ our Lord. Amen.[3]

Singing like a Harlot

> The Church of Christ in every age
> beset by change but Spirit led,
> Must claim and test its heritage
> and keep on rising from the dead.[4]

This hymn also hails from the quotable Fred Pratt Green. We Anglicans have a rich choral tradition, and it is worthy of being of being claimed and treasured, tended and taught. Trained choirs can help to bring great beauty, reverence,

---

3. Royal School of Church Music, Oxford Choristers' Prayer, http://www.rscm-oxford.org.uk/choristers'%20prayer.htm. Retrieved August 29, 2017.

4. "The Church of Christ in Every Age," *Wonder, Love, and Praise,* hymn 779.

and majesty by singing from this vast repertoire, and we can be genuinely inspired hearing poetry set to music by "the greats."

As the text suggests, we must also test that heritage, to make sure that it is helping us to rise from the dead, and not sealing us "in the stone-cold tomb."[5] Choirs and their leaders would do well to redouble efforts to focus on the song of the gathered, which is of paramount importance, at least in the thinking of the authors of this book. We must engage and empower the faithful in "singing psalms, hymns, spiritual songs," as Paul writes to the churches at Ephesus and Colossi.

Such singing helps to gather us in and send us out. It punctuates our liturgy in response to readings. It teaches us the historic faith of our forebears and breaks new ground in how we think of ourselves as a Church. It brings comfort in times of mourning, and joy at times of celebration. It revives old memories, and provides fodder for new ones. Ultimately it strengthens the church to be its best self; the living, breathing, singing, dying and rising body of Christ.

Years ago, we were having a conversation about the power of music, and the fact that doing some things outside the tradition, while seemingly unorthodox, had a powerful effect on members of our congregation. We had sung "In the Garden" at a funeral, and people responded with robust singing and tears. Hearts were opened, and lives

---

5. We Three Kings of Orient Are," *The Hymnal 1982,* hymn 128.

were changed in some small way. This kind of singing was something the church could offer while still maintaining the strong traditions received over the centuries. It reminded us of the ministry of Rahab, a "woman with a past" whose life was spared in the destruction of Jericho, because of her clever and subversive willingness to hide the spies of Israel. This not only enabled Israel to be victorious, but it was a sign that God can use any of us for good, even if we have a past!

That led Jeff to announce to Dent, "You are the poster child for St. Rahab the Harlot. Making a deposit in peoples' emotional bank accounts can work for good." First, we laughed. Then we took it to heart. Rahab had something to teach us and the church.

There now exists a Society of St. Rahab the Harlot, a group of slightly subversive musicians, clergy, and artists who are committed to the life of the church as a life of love and risk and adventure, who know and cherish the tradition and use it well, and who also introduce new things to shake up our congregations. We meet on a semi-regular basis to make music, plan liturgies, and bring new life, joy, inclusivity, and vitality to worship. A hymn that captures our mission might be this one:

> As newborn stars were stirred to song when all things
>   came to be,
> As Miriam and Moses sang when Israel was set free,

So music bursts unbidden forth when God-filled hearts
  rejoice
To waken awe and gratitude and give mute faith a voice.[6]

We want—no, we expect the church to burst forth in song in response to God's unfailing love for us. We expect that song to teach us how to keep on rising from the dead. We expect that song to carry us, to send us, to expel us into the world carrying a message of hope: that God is living right here in our midst, as close as our next breath.

GO DEEPER . . .

1. Is any hymn or religious song particularly meaningful to you? What are the words? What is the tune? Why does this song affect you so powerfully?

2. What messages did you hear about singing or making music, as a child? How do those messages affect you today?

---

6. "As Newborn Stars Were Stirred to Song," *Wonder, Love and Praise,* hymn 788.

Chapter 7

Gathered
for the Bath

In the last parish where we served together, on the east side of Seattle, we celebrated baptisms with great care. As in any parish through the years, we had the great gift of celebrating the baptisms of children and entire families. Perhaps because of the Northwest's thoroughly de-churched culture, we had more than our share often of adults, including young adults often generations away from any religious commitment, people who had discovered the Christian faith and who had chosen to make it their own way of life.

One of those young adults had a revelation during his preparation for baptism. He looked at our old font, which was not very large, and said, "You know, that's not quite big enough. My whole life has been turned upside down, and I think we need more water than that will hold." So an engineer-turned-carpenter in the congregation made a baptismal pool. He took a black, round pond liner and made a beautiful eight-sided oak surround for it. Filled with water a couple of feet deep, it was beautiful. Babies could be held over it as we poured water over them, and adults knelt in it to be liberally doused. It sat on the floor in front of the altar, in the middle of the aisle where you could not miss it.

On Pentecost Sunday the year we first used this pool, we had celebrated the baptisms of a bunch of children and adults. There were bagpipes and incense and banners and red balloons. The sun even came out, and this was Seattle, where the clouds do not part very often. As the final hymn began, the dove banner, cross, and candles started to lead us all out, the choir falling in right behind. You have to picture this: The church was set up with the organ and choir area right behind the altar, so in processions, the choir, walking two by two, would split to walk around the altar platform.

> Pentecost was originally a Jewish feast offering the first fruits of the harvest to God. The earliest Christians turned it into a celebration of the Spirit of Christ, God's first gift to us. In the Christian year, Pentecost is the culmination of the whole Easter season.

On this Pentecost Sunday, as the choir processed out, when the third pair of singers split to come back together in front of the altar, one member of the pair was not looking where he was going. His head was thrown back in song as he belted the closing hymn. He couldn't miss the font/pool.

With a spectacular splash, he went in head first. It is amazing how far water will travel when a fully grown adult man, wearing several yards of vestments, belly flops into it.

Diving in to Baptism

In some ways, it may seem strange to leave thinking about baptism until now, toward the end of this book. We've tried to make the point that the almost universal practice of the Christian community has been to insist that baptism is the entrance to the Christian life, that it incorporates new Christians into the Body of Christ and makes them living limbs and members of the risen Jesus. But the vision at the heart of the Episcopal Church's way of worshiping is that these are not simply things that happen occasionally in church—together they are a way of living.

Holy Baptism is a way of life, a lifelong journey of falling headfirst into the life of Jesus himself, and thus being formed into his image and likeness. This journey, like real life itself, is full of successes and failures, stops and starts, triumphs and tragedies. Sometimes the baptized life is a mess. But if we want to follow Christ we dive in anyway. We make following Jesus our daily life.

Nowhere is this more explicit than in the liturgical form called the **Baptismal Covenant**, located on pages 304 and 305 of the Book of Common Prayer. It represents a kind of rule of life, a set of commitments that over a lifetime will make habitual the essential practices of the Christian faith.

At the celebration of a baptism, the people to be baptized (or the parents and godparents of a child too young to answer) are asked questions that have been posed for centuries to those about to enter the waters of baptism.

The Reality of Evil

In something like a prelude to the Baptismal Covenant, the celebrant asks the candidates if they renounce the power of evil in this world and in their lives. "Do you renounce Satan and all the spiritual forces of wickedness that rebel against God? Do you renounce the evil powers of this world which corrupt and destroy the creatures of God? Do you renounce all sinful desires that draw you from the love of God?" The answer is always, "I renounce them."[1]

These questions are a frank admission of the reality of evil. The language may sound curious to modern ears—especially when we speak of Satan and spiritual forces—but this is simply the Bible's language for a reality we know all too much about.

Who could deny that something is amiss in this world? People suffer from terrible illnesses, natural disasters strike with sudden randomness, accidents and acts of terror are standard fare in the news. In the ancient world, demonic activity was assumed to be responsible for many of these ills. Today, we may describe their causes differently, but

---

1. BCP, 302.

their existence and power to wound us is still fundamentally a mystery.

> St. Paul wrote: "I do not understand my own actions. For I do not do what I want, but I do the very thing I hate." (Rom. 7:15)

The evil powers of this world might also bring to mind the "isms" that infect society: racism, sexism, ageism, homophobia—all those tendencies in us that turn other human beings into labels instead of human persons made in the image of God. And the sinful desires that keep us from accepting the fullness of God's love in our lives is an experience common to us all. This is the vexing issue of why we persist in doing the very things that we know are bad for us and our endless capacity for hurting other people, perhaps most mysteriously our capacity to hurt the people who are closest to us, our families and friends.

Turning to the Good

After the candidates for baptism renounce the power of these realities in their lives and commit themselves to refuse to give these things any more power over their lives than they already have, then they are asked to turn to the good. For Christians, the ultimate good has a name, Jesus. If you want to see what a whole and holy human being looks like,

> Ancient descriptions of baptisms tell of candidates making these promises physically turning from facing the west to the east, toward the rising sun and toward the direction from which it was believed Christ would return.

look no further than Jesus. "Do you turn to Jesus Christ and accept him as your savior?" we ask. "Do you put your whole trust in his grace and love? Do you promise to follow him as your Savior and Lord?" These promises stand at the heart of the Christian **faith**. They point to the Christian faith as a way of life rather than a set of abstract ideas about God, a robust way of living "no longer for ourselves alone," as one version of the Great Thanksgiving puts it.

When we make these promises at baptism, they remind us that too much of Christianity has become a matter of thinking about certain vague and spiritual things that do not really make much of a difference in anyone's daily life. The writer Frederick Buechner observed that the word "spirit has come to mean something pale and shapeless, like an unmade bed."[2] We believe that faith is not something you *have*. It is not just having certain pious thoughts. Faith is something you *do*. It is a way of behaving in the face of life's challenges and joys.

Like forgiveness or love, the word "faith" makes a much better verb than a noun. It is not uncommon to hear people in church from time to time worry about their faith when they have trouble feeling things they imagine good Christians ought to feel. "I must not be a very good Christian, because I just don't know how I could ever forgive her for what she's done!" That is what happens when we believe faith is primarily a matter of feeling certain ways.

---

2. Frederick Buechner, *Wishful Thinking* (San Francisco: Harper & Row, 1973), 90.

This sometimes comes up in relation to the word "love," too. Especially in the context of celebrating the lifelong commitment of two persons to one another in marriage, we are not talking about love as a feeling, which comes and goes. We speak of love as a decision. There will be times when the couple will feel starry eyed about one another, and there are definitely times when they will not, but even and especially at those times it will be important to remember that they can continue to choose to love one another, that is to put the good of the other ahead of their own.

Faith is the decision to act in this world on the basis of trust that ultimately God intends only good for us. In baptism, we commit ourselves to practice these decisions, to practice living on the basis of them. This is why we prefer to speak of the Christian faith as a set of practices rather than a performance.

The promises to follow Christ, to put our whole trust in him and to follow him as savior and lord, are radically counter-cultural commitments. The biblical scholar Walter Brueggemann has said that the decline of institutional Christianity has nothing to do with the labels of "liberal" or "conservative," but rather "with giving up on the faith and discipline of our Christian baptism and settling for a common, generic . . . identity that is part patriotism, part consumerism, part violence, and part affluence."[3]

---

3. Walter Brueggemann, *A Way Other than Our Own* (Louisville: John Knox Press, 2017), 3.

Dominant North American culture preaches to us in a million and one ways that we can save ourselves, provide our own security, guarantee our own happiness. We are surrounded by powerful messages that if we only look good enough, perform well enough, have enough money in the bank, buy the right things, then we will be safe. On the national and global stage these assumptions have massive consequences for the planet. Our reliance on military force, the proliferation of handguns, the dependence of our economy on conspicuous consumption and inequality—these can all be seen as examples of the way we put our trust in things other than Christ.

We Can't Do It Alone

After these promises to renounce the power of evil and to follow the way of Christ, comes the Baptismal Covenant itself.

First, the whole congregation is asked if they will do everything in their power to support the candidates in their life in Christ. This is an acknowledgment of the essentially corporate nature of the Christian faith. We cannot do this alone. An ancient saying among Christians has been this: One Christian is no Christian. We hold this faith together.

In a way, asking the whole congregation to stand and join in the Baptismal Covenant is a reflection of what we believe to be true of God's own nature. To confess that God is one *and* three persons in perfect communion is to say that in some way God is relationship. If we are made in the image of God, then we find our most authentic selves only in relationship too.

The Baptismal Covenant begins with a question and answer form of the Creed: Do you believe in God the Father? Jesus Christ his only Son? God the Holy Spirit? Together with those coming to the water of baptism, everyone in the gathered body confesses our faith and trust in this Triune God.

After the Creed come what we like to call the "So-What Questions." These five simple questions are a way of expressing our commitment to respond in very practical ways to the faith we have professed in God. They are about putting our faith into practice and making real in our lives what we have professed by our faith.

Although they have to do with commitments and actions that could be recognized as central to any group of Christian believers, they occupy a particularly important place in the life of the Episcopal Church. Since this particular form of these promises was adopted by our church in the 1970s, they have had a profound impact on the way we think of practicing the Christian faith.

In Episcopal churches the Baptismal Covenant is repeated not only at the celebration of every baptism, but also at other occasions throughout the year when we recommit ourselves to this way of life.

1. The first question is: *"Will you continue in the apostles' teaching and fellowship, in the breaking of bread, and in the prayers?"* In other words, "Will you keep going to church?" We begin this set of questions by promising to stay with the community of the friends of Jesus who are trying to realize the implications of putting their trust in him. The Christian faith is irreducibly communal. As Mary Gray-Reeves, Bishop of the Diocese of El Camino Real, puts it, "Community is the technology of the Holy Spirit." Together is the one reliable way we will know the presence and power of God.

2. The second question follows: *"Will you persevere in resisting evil, and, whenever you fall into sin, repent and return to the Lord?"* Notice this question does not say, "*If* you sin." No, it says when you do. In the Episcopal Church, we are very honest about the inevitability of sin, of turning from God's love and acceptance of us and about our capacity to wound our neighbor. At our best we are equally clear about the love and forgiveness of God. Every sin that we have ever or will ever commit has been forgiven. That is the good news Jesus came to make real. We have heard it said that the gospel of Jesus can be boiled down to one sentence: "You can screw it up but you can't blow it." We humans mess it up all the time—sin is all too real a power in our lives—and yet the power of God's love is greater. There is nothing anyone can do to make God stop loving them. God has decided to love us, to forgive us, to heal us. All that is left to us to do is to open our hearts to receive the gift.

3. The third question: *"Will you proclaim by word and example the Good News of God in Christ?"* This question does not ask us to knock on our neighbor's door and drill them with questions about accepting Jesus Christ as their personal Lord and Savior. Episcopalians are not known for that kind of **evangelism**. In fact, there are lots of members of the Episcopal Church who blanch at the word evangelism because in popular usage it has come to mean a kind of hard sales tactic. We do not think there is anything inherently wrong with that kind of witnessing; it just does not seem to be especially effective. Many people are simply put off by attempts to talk them into believing things about God. This question in the Baptismal Covenant asks us to share the good news by word and example. In other words, it asks us to *be* the good news we preach. Who needs to hear some good news? And how could we embody that news for them? If they ask, "Why are you being so good to me?" we should be ready to tell them, "I'm a Christian. It's what we do." God has been good beyond imagining to us—we can do nothing less than share some of that experience with others.

4. The fourth question pushes us deeper into the implications of sharing God's love. *"Will you seek and serve Christ in all persons, loving your neighbor as yourself?"* Importantly, this question does not ask us to like or enjoy our neighbor. As we have discussed earlier in this book, when Christians use the word love, we are not talking primarily about a feeling. We are talking about a decision, a commitment to practice putting the good of the other before our own. This question might well be asking us to love our neighbor, to look for the presence of Christ particularly in the neighbor who is foreign to us. In the neighbor who threatens and frightens us. In the neighbor who has injured us. Jesus was disconcertingly clear when he told us to love our enemies. It is part of the lifelong journey of the Christian life to grapple with questions of just how to love those we find difficult or troublesome. Here is another reason we need each other to figure it all out.

5. The fifth question extends this question of loving our neighbor into the realm of social, public, and even political life. *"Will you strive for justice and peace among all people, and respect the dignity of every human being?"* This question might almost be summarized by asking: Will you vote and engage in political life? Christians promise to take their place in working for a world, a society more like the one God wants to see, a world in which everyone will have what they need, and not as a matter of charity. That may be as close as we can get to shorthand description of what the Bible means by the word "justice."

People sometimes say that they want to keep politics out of church. But we might as well say we want to keep Jesus out of church. Politics is simply the art of living together. It has to do with the way our institutions, governments and policies ensure the cohesion, good order, and effective functioning of society. The Bible has plenty to say about these matters. The prophets in the Hebrew Scriptures reserve their harshest criticisms for those in power who abuse the poor and the helpless. In his letter to a young leader in the church named Timothy, the apostle Paul writes to say that Christians should pray for those in authority for the sake of the common good (1 Tim. 2:1–3). Since then, there has been a long history among Christians of reflecting on the implications of their faith for the good of the whole community.[4]

The answer to each of these questions is "I will, with God's help." These commitments are personal. We make them as individuals, but as individuals who stand together in community and always relying on the power of God to equip us to keep them. Christians call this power "grace." We admit that ultimately we can do nothing operating under only our own steam.

What Love Looks Like

The service for Holy Baptism now proceeds to the water itself. We have already said some things about the power of water as a symbol, a sign of cleansing and birth. We have compared the passing of Israel through the sea to freedom and new identity, with the passover of Jesus himself through the final chaos of death to resurrection. All of these images are woven together in a prayer of thanksgiving for the gift of water. It is said or sung over the water in the baptismal

---

4. These words appear in the Book of Common Prayer beginning on pages 293 (the Easter Vigil service), page 417 (confirmation), and page 304 (baptism).

font, the water through which the candidates for baptism will soon pass.

This is a powerful prayer full of rich and evocative images. It is all the more so when the water over which it is prayed is abundant, in a vessel large enough to hold lots of it, maybe even in a pool on the floor. It might even be "living" water, moving around in the font by means of a fountain or water running into it. The instructions in the Book of Common Prayer direct the bishop or priest who is praying these words to touch the water at one point. That is at least one way to make the water move just a little.

> The 1662 Book of Common Prayer, still the official prayer book of the Church of England, was formalized after more than a century of revisions made to the original 1549 Book of Common Prayer amidst the turmoil of the English Reformation and the English Civil War.

Now comes the bath itself. The word baptize originally meant "to dip" and the earliest Christian practice was to baptize people through immersion, although exceptions were made when there wasn't sufficient water available. The 1662 prayer book of the Church of England gives this instruction for the baptism of infants:

Then the Priest shall take the Child into his hands, and shall say to the Godfathers and Godmothers, Name this Child. And then naming it after them (if they shall certify him that the Child may well endure it) he shall dip it in the Water discreetly and warily, saying, N. I baptize thee in the Name of the Father, and of the Son, and of the Holy Ghost. Amen. But if they certify that the Child is weak, it shall suffice to pour Water upon it . . . .

On the other hand, the instruction in the 1979 Book of Common Prayer says simply, "Each candidate is presented by name to the Celebrant . . . who then immerses, or pours water upon, the candidate . . . ."

While most baptisms in the Episcopal Church are still those of infants and the most common way of baptizing them is by pouring over their heads, the clear and traditional preference is for immersion. We are convinced that the significance of baptism as rebirth into a completely new life in the image of Christ is most richly experienced when it is the baptism of an adult who has been prepared for it with the participation of a whole community. When such a baptism is in enough water to suggest bathing and birthing, dying and rising, the impact on the rest of the congregation can be powerful. The baptism of an infant or a child, of course, can also be a moving sign of the love and mercy of God who brings us into life without any choice or effort on our part. Life, like salvation in Christ, is all pure gift.

After being washed, the newly baptized person is anointed with **chrism**, perfumed olive oil signifying the royal priesthood of Jesus. The way of referring to baptism as "christening" derives from this anointing. The word "Christ" is not Jesus's last name, but it is a theological title. *Christos* in

Greek is the translation of the Hebrew word for Messiah; they both mean "anointed one." Anointing with oil is an ancient and biblical sign of designating a prophet or a king. Jesus is the One anointed by God as the Savior, the Messiah, and those who are baptized—made members of his body— are living images, icons of Christ. Rising from the waters of the font, the newly baptized is a living sign participating in the resurrection of Christ rising before our very eyes.

> By long tradition the blessing of **chrism** is something done only by the bishop, a reminder of a time when the bishop of a diocese was the presider at all baptisms and a sign of the unity in Christ of all the people of the diocese. In some dioceses, the blessing of chrism happens once a year, often during Holy Week, just in time for the celebration of baptisms at the Great Vigil of Easter.

Significantly, the anointing is usually done by making the sign of the cross on the forehead. We do not sign the newly baptized with a smiley face, but with the cross. We tell them the truth: This is going to hurt. Living involves pain. Anything approaching being worthy of the word "love" contains within itself at least the possibility of agony. Jesus's crucifixion is the ultimate demonstration of it. To contemplate the total vulnerability of Jesus willingly enduring the cross is to behold the mystery of love. This is what love looks like.

We like to say that learning to live the baptized life is reality therapy. The Christian faith does not promise to rescue us from the hard realities of being human. Jesus did not come to fish us out of the human condition; he came to enter it with us and so to transform it. Pain and suffering are not the whole story. But just as people in addiction recovery discover, there is no way around addiction, pain, heartache, death, but there is a way *through*. That is the meaning of Christ's death and resurrection.

Becoming Outsiders

In ancient descriptions of baptisms at Easter, the newly baptized were greeted with lavish signs of reverence, just as Christ himself might be reverenced. And they were— and still are—welcomed with joy to the Lord's table. The culmination of baptism is receiving Holy Communion, ideally during the same liturgy. In the Episcopal Church, this applies to the newly baptized of any age, infants as well as adults.

The decision of an adult to profess the Christian faith and receive the sacrament of baptism demonstrates the gift and responsibility of responding, as humans with free will, to the freely bestowed gift of God's grace. The baptism of an infant is a sign of the infinite goodness of God whose gift of life and new life in Christ is for us pure, unearned grace. In the sacrament of Christ's body and blood we receive the very thing we have become. As the words of the invitation to Holy Communion put it: "The Gifts of God for the People of God." That includes us all.

And in the same way we are all gathered into the one body of Christ, so we are all given a share in the mission of Christ. We share in the work of Jesus, the ministry of reconciling all people to a right relationship with one another and with God. Immediately after their washing and anointing, the newly baptized are welcomed with profound and challenging words: "We receive you into the household of God. Confess the faith of Christ crucified, proclaim his resurrection, and share with us in his eternal priesthood."

The newly baptized are welcomed to join in the celebration of the Eucharist with the oily cross of Christ still shining on their foreheads, the sign of the costly work of reconciliation. One of our colleagues suggests that we should balance our view of baptism as a sacrament of inclusion with the perspective that it is also a sacrament of expulsion. We are baptized to be excluded from many of the assumptions of privilege and comfort that being "included" might mean. We are not included in the embrace of God for the sake of ourselves, but like Jesus we live so that others might know that embrace too, to live and act in this world so that ultimately there may be no more inside and outside.

Just as the Holy Spirit drove Jesus out into the desert after his baptism, scholar Roger Ferlo says our baptism "makes us all outsiders, expelled from the center to inhabit the margins, driven by the Spirit out of our places of safety—whether it's our fishing boats or our churches, our racial prejudices or our economic comfort—to make common cause with the poor and the isolated, the refugee and the captive."[5] This is the baptized life.

We are gathered by Christ through the power of the Holy Spirit into the embrace of God, not for ourselves, but to be sent out to the world with our arms wide open. We are called to be a sacrament of God's embrace. We are called to be agents of God's grace in this fearful, wounded world. The practice of worship in the Episcopal Church has this—nothing more and nothing less—as its aim.

GO DEEPER ...

1. If you have been baptized, how old were you? Have you had the opportunity to reaffirm your baptismal promises? If so, what impact did this have on your life?

2. Of the five promises at the heart of the Baptismal Covenant, which presents the greatest challenge to you? Which most shapes your life?

5. Roger Ferlo, "Baptism Makes Us All Outsiders," January 24, 2014, https://www.bexleyseabury.edu/baptism-makes-us-all-outsiders/. Retrieved on August 29, 2017.

Chapter 8

Gathered like We Mean It

We like the liberating inscription found on many a birthday card: "Dance like nobody's watching." It seems to us that in too many church services, everyone is conscious that everyone else (maybe including God) is watching, ready to take note of every deviation from the norm, every misstep or mistake.

But the liturgy is not a performance. The liturgy is an art form that is not meant to entertain or impress or edify or instruct. It is a corporate act of the people of God that aims to change us, to draw us out of our self-conscious preoccupations and deeper into the mystery of the dying and rising love of God for us and for this world. It is an encounter with God's own presence.

Granted, it is not always immediately clear that anything like this is happening in a typical church on a Sunday morning. Would a complete stranger to the Christian faith have any inkling of the vast mystery we gather to encounter here? The author Annie Dillard suggests the answer is no:

> On the whole, I do not find Christians, outside of the catacombs, sufficiently sensible of conditions. Does anyone have the foggiest idea what sort of power we so blithely invoke? Or, as I suspect, does no one believe a word of it? The churches are children playing on the floor with their chemistry sets, mixing up a batch of TNT to kill a Sunday morning. It is madness to wear ladies' straw hats and velvet hats to church; we should all be wearing crash helmets. Ushers should issue life preservers and signal flares; they should lash us to our pews. For the sleeping god may wake someday and take offense, or the waking god may draw us out to where we can never return.[1]

Dillard shocks us with her strong words, but maybe we—like that sleeping god—need to wake up. Our colleague Jim Steen often says the worst and most persistent sin the church continues to commit is to bore people. It is worth pondering.

What We Don't Say

The liturgy of the Book of Common Prayer is enacted in very formal services with professional quality choirs, incense,

---

1. Annie Dillard, *Teaching a Stone to Talk: Expeditions and Encounters* (New York: Harper & Row, 1982), 40–41.

and elaborate vestments, in informal gatherings around a simple altar table with a couple of hymns, and in every setting in between. There are many choices of particular texts that might be used, from those found printed in the Book of Common Prayer itself to a number of "alternative" texts approved for use by the General Convention of the Episcopal Church.

While the texts and verbal images used to address God may be attention-grabbing, we believe a much more powerful factor in the experience of a given act of worship may well be the whole complex of non-verbal gestures and actions that accompany the words, including the music being sung or heard. The building itself where worship is being conducted may be the most powerful factor of all. If the building in which you are worshiping looks and feels like a Gothic cathedral with altar, clergy and choir at one far end of the building and the majority of people confined to fixed pews, that will be a very different experience than worshipping in a contemporary or renovated space with movable chairs that enable people and clergy to gather freely around an altar table in their midst.

Our conviction is that there are many valid architectural options, just as there are many styles of music appropriate to worship, many forms of visual arts, a whole range of gestures, processions, even fragrances to enliven worship. None of these things is an end to itself. The key to making effective use of any or all of them lies in the intention and planning with which they are deployed and the leaders' clarity about their purpose in supporting the whole point of a liturgical gathering.

If sacraments make visibly real what is already inwardly true, then the quality of the materials that make up the outward and visible sign matters very much. There is no doubt that God can use a tasteless, dry disk of wheat and flour to communicate the bread of heaven to God's people. Wouldn't the experience of that feeding be quite different if the material of the sacrament were a large, fragrant loaf baked by a member of the congregation, broken into fragments for everyone to share?

We have no misgivings that the baptism of a child accomplished by three drops of water passing through three inches of air absolutely incorporates that child into the Body of Christ. It will be a very different human experience if that baptism bathes the child or adult in plenty of water, maybe running water, enough to splash around in and even potentially dangerous. How better to make the point that this bath is a participation in the passing over of Christ from death to new life?

We long to see the perfumed oil used to anoint the newly baptized poured and massaged lovingly onto their foreheads as they are signed with the cross. A respected priest and teacher in the Episcopal Church, John Westerhoff, once said impishly: "We can continue to talk all we want to about baptism as a participation in the death and resurrection of Jesus, but no one ever drowned from being dribbled on."

What if all the members of our congregations engaged regularly in brief and inviting rehearsals so that everyone might join with gusto in the singing of new music? What if congregations were invited and taught to participate fully in the liturgy, not just in the spoken recitation of group texts, but in the full range of the "choreography" that belongs to them: bowing and kneeling and processing and making the sign of the cross and unashamedly raising their hands in prayer as their ancestors in the faith did?

Boggling the Mind

We suspect that part of the boredom too many people seem to equate with the services of the church comes from a lack of full, embodied engagement in worship. For many reasons, we have rendered the Christian faith into something that happens only from the ears up.

This may be why so many people in our time seem to have such trouble with the word "believe." We encounter people all the time who say that when it comes to the profession

> First set forth in 325 in the midst of theological controversies about the nature of the Trinity, the Nicene Creed is used in Eucharist on Sundays and feast days; the Apostles' Creed, developed from an early church question-and-answer profession of faith, is used in the celebration of Baptisms and in the Daily Office services of Morning and Evening Prayer.

of faith we call the **Creed**, they don't actually say it or they cross their fingers. When asked why, they sometimes sheepishly confess that they don't actually believe all that stuff. When they are asked what they mean by the word "believe," they usually talk about thinking that something is really true or at least plausible, even in demonstrable sense. But believing in that sense is not what the word creed (*credo* in Latin) means. *Cogito* (Latin for "to think") perhaps, but not *credo*. The word *credo* is related to the word for the heart.

What does this mean? It means the Creed is not a statement of intellectual assent as much as it is a love song. Its origins may have been in early Christian attempts to state clearly the church's understanding of the nature of God the Holy Trinity, but all any creed can do is to point in the direction of God. Any attempt to define God in a succinct formula is doomed to failure. One of the greatest Christian theologians of the early centuries, St. Augustine, said simply, "If you can understand it . . . it's not God."[2]

We wonder if the doctrine of the Trinity in some sense does for Christians what the absolute prohibition of visual images does for Jews and Muslims, namely guarding against the creation of idols. To speak of one God in three persons makes no ordinary sense on purpose. We have a way of imaging and praising God that boggles the mind. God is always more. We will never understand God, we can

---

2. St. Augustine, Sermon 52, 6, 16: PL 38, 360 and Sermon 117, 3, 5: PL 38, 663.

however with perfect confidence trust God. We can give God our hearts. The worship of the church helps us to practice doing just that.

God Doesn't Need Liturgy

We have worked with a professor named Michelle Buck at the Kellogg School at Northwestern University who teaches leadership to business and non-profit executives by teaching them the Argentine tango. It's not always an easy sell for those new to her class, but her point is a serious one. For the tango to "work," the leader has to have a partner who pushes back just enough. An essential tension is necessary if the dance is to be successful.

She says leaders need to get this knowledge into their bodies. They need to practice what this creative tension feels like so that when something similar inevitably comes up in their organizational life they will be prepared to work with it. It seems to us that something akin to this should be going on in the liturgical life of the church, for the sake of the mission of the church. The liturgy helps us to get the faith into our bodies, into our flesh and blood and bone.

We set a lavish welcome table because our mission is to meet the desperate hungers of the world. We welcome, wash, and anoint new members because our mission is to wash and tend the wounds of those who have no help or hope. We praise God together because God is simply God, the creator, the sustainer, the possibility of life itself. We are made in God's image and made for community, and our mission is to proclaim the goodness of God to a world that believes it has created and sustains itself and is therefore free to do to creation whatever it likes. We need to know what these things feel like. We need to practice them to be effective agents of God's mission of restoring all things to right relationship.

It is important to remember that God doesn't need liturgy. We do. In the Book of Common Prayer's form for the liturgy of Ash Wednesday, after a lengthy confession of sin, the bishop or priest assures the people of God's forgiveness and then says, "Therefore we beseech him to grant us true repentance and his Holy Spirit, that those things may please him which we do on this day . . . so that at the last we may come to his eternal joy; through Jesus Christ our Lord."[3] We naturally want to please God with our prayer, but we are not performing a pageant or a play so that God will notice and delight in us.

The Christian life does involve change and growth, some of it painful. In fact following Jesus leads us inexorably to the cross. So praying with a fierce tenderness, celebrating the sacraments with conviction, and making lavish use of the good things of creation—water, oil, bread, wine, reverent human touch, the power of communal song—we need these things, not just to be "good" Christian people, but to be fully human beings. In the society in which many of us

---

3. BCP, 269.

live now, connected electronically but increasingly isolated from face-to-face community, reckoning with social and economic shock and global climate change, we need the human arts of gathering. We need rituals that commit us to something greater than ourselves, that speak to us of our utter reliance on the power of God working in and through us. We need these things to equip us to take up the cross and to find the only real life worth living.

GO DEEPER . . .

1. What styles of worship have you found particularly moving or engaging? What was happening?

2. Have you ever been bored in worship? What was happening in worship that contributed to that experience?

Further Reading

Bangert, Mark Paul. *Leading the Church's Song*. Minneapolis: Augsburg Fortress, 1998.

Bradshaw, Paul F., and Maxwell E. Johnson. *The Eucharistic Liturgies: Their Evolution and Interpretation*. Collegeville, MN: Liturgical Press, 2012.

Foley, Edward. *From Age to Age, How Christians Have Celebrated the Eucharist*. Collegeville, MN: Liturgical Press, 2008.

Hamilton, Reid, and Stephen Rush. *Better Get It in Your Soul: What Liturgists Can Learn from Jazz*. New York: Church Publishing, 2008.

Hatchett, Marion. *Commentary on the American Prayer Book*. New York: HarperCollins, 1995.

Hovda, Robert. *Strong, Loving, and Wise*. Collegeville, MN: Liturgical Press, 1976.

Larson-Miller, Lizette. *Sacramentality Renewed: Contemporary Conversations in Sacramental Theology*. Collegeville, MN: Liturgical Press, 2016.

Lee, Jeffrey D. *Opening the Prayer Book*. Cambridge, MA: Cowley Publications, 1999.

Malloy, Patrick. *Celebrating the Eucharist*. New York: Church Publishing, 2007.

Mitchell, Leonel, and Ruth Meyers. *Praying Shapes Believing: A Theological Commentary on the Book of Common Prayer.* New York: Seabury Books, 2016.

Morris, Clayton. *Holy Hospitality: Worship and the Baptismal Covenant*. New York: Church Publishing, 2005.

Music that Makes Community (curator of paperless music). www.musicthatmakescommunity.org.

Reynolds, Simon. *Table Manners, Liturgical Leadership for the Mission of the Church.* London: SCM Press, 2014.

Rideout, Marti. *All Things Necessary: A Practical Guide for Episcopal Church Musicians*. New York: Morehouse Publishing, 2012.

Roberts, William Bradley. *Music and Vital Congregations: A Practical Guide for Clergy*. New York: Church Publishing, 2009.

Smith, George Wayne. *Admirable Simplicity*. New York: Church Publishing, 1996.

Spellers, Stephanie. *Radical Welcome: Embracing God, the Other and Transformation*. New York: Church Publishing, 2006.

Weil, Louis. *Liturgical Sense*. New York: Seabury Books, 2013.

Weil, Louis. *A Theology of Worship*. Cambridge, MA: Cowley Publications, 2002.